CH00655941

THE LITTLE BOOK OF
CATS

On some grave business,
Soft and slow
Along the garden paths you go
With bold and burning eyes,
Or stand with twitching tail to mark
What starts and rustles in the dark
Among the peonies.

A. C. BENSON

Animals are not brethren, they are not underlings; they are other nations, caught with ourselves in the net of life and time.

HENRY BESTON

The Pope's Cat

I have as companion a big greyish red cat
with black stripes across it. It was born in
the Vatican, in the Raphael loggia. Leo XII
brought it up in a fold of his robes where I
had often looked at it enviously when the
Pontiff gave me an audience.... It was called
"the Pope's cat." In this capacity, it used to
enjoy the special consideration of pious
ladies. I am trying to make it forget exile,
the Sistine Chapel, the sun on Michelangelo's
cupola, where it used to walk, far above
the earth.

VICOMTE DE CHATEAUBRIAND

The soul of another is darkness, and a cat's
soul more than most.

ANTON CHEKHOV

Dr. Johnson's Hodge

I shall never forget the indulgence with which he treated Hodge, his cat; for whom he used to go out and buy oysters.... I recollect him one day scrambling up on Dr. Johnson's breast, apparently with much satisfaction, while my friend, smiling and half-whistling, rubbed his back and pulled him by the tail; and when I observed he was a fine cat, saying, "Why, yes, Sir, but I have had cats whom I liked better than this." And then as if perceiving Hodge to be out of countenance adding, "But he is a very fine cat, very fine cat indeed."

JAMES BOSWELL

To a Cat

Stately, kindly lordly friend,
    Condescend
Here to sit by me, and turn
Glorious eyes that smile and burn,
Golden eyes, love's lustrous meed,
On the golden page I read.

All your wondrous wealth of hair
    Dark and fair,
Silken-shaggy, soft and bright
As the clouds and beams of night,
Pays my reverent hand's caress
Back with friendlier gentleness.

Dogs may fawn on all and some
    As they come;
You, a friend of loftier mind,
Answer friends alone in kind.
Just your foot upon my hand
Softly bids it understand.

Wild on woodland ways your sires
    Flashed like fires:
Fair as flame and fierce and fleet
As with wings on wingless feet
Shone and sprang your mother, free,
Bright and brave as wind or sea.

Free and proud and glad as they,
    Here today
Rests or roams their radiant child,
Vanquished not, but reconciled,
Free from curb of aught above
Save the lovely curb of love.

ALGERNON CHARLES SWINBURNE

From "Jubilate Deo"

For I will consider my Cat Jeoffry.
For he is the servant of the Living God, duly
and daily serving him.
For at the first glance of the glory of God in
the East he worships in his way.
For is this done by wreathing his body seven
times round with elegant quickness.
For then he leaps up to catch the musk,
which is the blessing of God upon his
prayer.
For he rolls upon prank to work it in.
For having done duty and received blessing
he begins to consider himself.
For this he performs in ten degrees.
For first he looks upon his forepaws to see if
they are clean.
For secondly he kicks up behind to clear
away there.
For thirdly he works it upon stretch with the
forepaws extended.

For fourthly he sharpens his paws by wood.
For fifthly he washes himself.
For sixthly he rolls upon wash.
For seventhly he fleas himself, that he may
    not be interrupted upon the beat.
For eighthly he rubs himself against a post.
For ninthly he looks up for his instructions.
For tenthly he goes in quest of food.
For having considered God and himself he
    will consider his neighbour.
For if he meets another cat he will kiss her in
    kindness.
For when he takes his prey he plays with it to
    give it a chance.
For one mouse in seven escapes by his
    dallying.
For when his day's work is done his business
    more properly begins.
For he keeps the Lord's watch in the night
    against the adversary.
For he counteracts the powers of darkness by
    his electrical skin and glaring eyes.
For he counteracts the Devil, who is death,

by brisking about the life.

For in his morning orisons he loves the sun
and the sun loves him.

For he is of the tribe of Tiger.

For the Cherub Cat is a term of the Angel
Tiger.

For he has the subtlety and hissing of a
serpent, which in goodness he suppresses.

For he will not do destruction, if he is well-
fed, neither will he spit without
provocation.

For he purrs in thankfulness, when God tells
him he's a good Cat.

And he is an instrument for the children to
learn benevolence upon.

For every house is incomplete without him
and a blessing is lacking in the spirit.

CHRISTOPHER SMART

Those who play with cats must expect to be scratched.

MIGUEL DE CERVANTES

It is as easy to hold quicksilver between your finger and thumb as to keep a cat who means to escape.

ANDREW LANG

If a fish is the movement of water embodied, given shape, then cat is a diagram and pattern of subtle air.

DORIS LESSING
FROM *PARTICULARLY CATS*

The Cat and the Moon

The cat went here and there
And the moon spun round like a top,
And the nearest kin of the moon,
The creeping cat, looked up.
Black Minnaloushe stared at the moon,
For, wander and wail as he would,
The pure cold light in the sky
Troubled his animal blood.
Minnaloushe runs in the grass
Lifting his delicate feet.
Do you dance, Minnaloushe, do you dance?
When two close kindred meet,
What better than call a dance?
Maybe the moon may learn,
Tired of that courtly fashion,
A new dance turn.
Minnaloushe creeps through the grass
From moonlit place to place,
The sacred moon overhead
Has taken a new phase.

Does Minnaloushe know that his pupils
Will pass from change to change,
And that from round to crescent,
From crescent to round they range?
Minnaloushe creeps through the grass
Alone, important and wise,
And lifts to the changing moon
His changing eyes.

WILLIAM BUTLER YEATS

From "The Long-Cat"

Show your hands!" my mother used to say to him, and thereupon he surrendered to her a long front paw, adept at every kind of mischief, with pads as hard as a road parched with drought.

"Have you been opening a melon?"

I dare say he understood. His gentle yellow eyes met Sido's penetrating look, but since his innocence was only assumed, he could not help squinting a little.

"Yes, you have opened a melon. And I expect it was the pretty little one I had my eye on, the one that looked like a globe with yellow continents and green seas." She released the long paw which fell back limp and expressionless.

"That deserves a good slap," said I.

COLETTE

Let take a cat and foster hym well with milk
And tender flesh and make his couche of silk,
And let hym see a mouse go by the wall,
Anon he waiveth milk and meat and all,
And every deynty that is in the house,
Such appetite hath he to eat a mouse.

GEOFFREY CHAUCER
FROM "THE MANCIPLE'S TALE,"
THE CANTERBURY TALES

The most domestic cat, which has lain on a rug all her days, appears quite at home in the woods, and, by her sly and stealthy behavior, proves herself more native there than the inhabitants.

HENRY DAVID THOREAU

On Mrs Reynolds's Cat

Cat! who hast pass'd thy grand
  climacteric,
How many mice and rats hast in thy days
Destroy'd—How many titbits stolen? Gaze
With those bright languid segments green
  and prick
Those velvet ears—but pr'ythee do not stick
Thy latent talons in me—and upraise
Thy gentle mew—and tell me all thy frays
Of fish and mice, and rats and tender chick.
Nay, look not down, nor lick thy dainty
  wrists—
For all thy wheezy asthma,—and for all
Thy tail's tip is nick'd off—and though the
  fists
Of many a maid have given thee many a maul,
Still is that fur as soft as when the lists
In youth thou enter'dst on glass-bottled wall.

JOHN KEATS

From "The Cat That Walked by Himself," Just So Stories

He will kill mice and he will be kind to babies when he is in the house, just as long as they do not pull his tail too hard. But when he has done that, and between times, and when the moon gets up and night comes, he is the Cat that Walks by Himself, and all places are alike to him. Then he goes out to the Wet Wild Woods or up the Wet Wild Trees or on the Wet Wild Roofs, waving his tail and walking by his wild lone.

RUDYARD KIPLING

The cat never even looked at them. With deliberation it stiffened its legs, so that it seemed to stand on its toes, flung up its tail straight as a poker—and walked disdainfully away from the firemen, leaving only the bright adieu beneath its tail.

**WILLIAM SANSOM
FROM "CAT UP A TREE,"
*AMONG THE DAHLIAS AND OTHER STORIES***

Of all animals, the cat alone attains to the contemplative life. He regards the wheel of existence from without, like the Buddha.

ANDREW LANG

Animals are such agreeable friends—they ask no questions; they pass no criticisms.

GEORGE ELIOT

Fantasy
and Fun

The Owl and the Pussy-Cat

The Owl and the Pussy-Cat went to sea
In a beautiful pea-green boat;
They took some honey, and plenty of money
Wrapped up in a five-pound note.
The Owl looked up to the moon above,
And sang to a small guitar:
"O lovely Pussy! O Pussy, my love!
What a beautiful Pussy you are,—you are,
What a beautiful Pussy you are!"

Pussy said to the owl: "You elegant fowl!
How charmingly sweet you sing!
O let us be married—too long we have
    tarried—
But what shall we do for a ring?"
They sailed away for a year and a day
To the land where the Bong-tree grows,
And there in a wood, a Piggy-wig stood
With a ring in the end of his nose,—his nose,
With a ring in the end of his nose.

Dear Pig, are you willing to sell for one
  shilling
Your ring?" Said the Piggy, "I will."
So they took it away, and were married next
  day
By the turkey who lives on the hill.
They dined upon mince and slices of quince,
Which they ate with a runcible spoon,
And hand in hand on the edge of the sand
They danced by the light of the moon,—the
  moon,
They danced by the light of the moon.

EDWARD LEAR

The War of the Roses

Huff the talbot and our cat Tib
They took up sword and shield,
Tib for the red rose, Huff for the white,
To fight upon Bosworth Field.

Oh, it was dreary that night to bury
Those doughty warriors dead,
Under a white rose brave dog Huff,
And fierce Tib under a red.

Low lay Huff and long may he lie!
But our Tib took little harm:
He was up and away at dawn of day
With the rose-bush under his arm.

ROBERT GRAVES

The contents of your letter are very pleasant and very welcome, and I thank you for them, sincerely, If I can find a photograph of my "Tammany" and her kittens, I will enclose it in this. One of them likes to be crammed into a corner pocket of the billiard table—which he fits as snugly as does a finger in a glove and then he watches the game (and obstructs it) by the hour, and spoils many a shot by putting out his paw and changing the direction of a passing ball. Whenever a ball is in his arms, or so close to him that it cannot be played upon without risk of hurting him, the player is privileged to remove it to any of the 3 spots that chances to be vacant.

Sincerely yours,

S. L. CLEMENS (MARK TWAIN),
FROM A LETTER TO MRS. PATTERSON, 1908

A Music Hall Song

A downy cove is our old tom cat,
Just turned thirty years old;
He eateth the lean, and leaveth the fat,
And won't touch his meals when too cold.
His food must be crumbled, and not decayed,
To pleasure his dainty whim,
But a turkey bone from the kitchen-maid
Is a very good meal for him.

Chorus:
Creeping over the tiles pit pat,
A downy cove is the old tom cat.

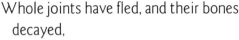

Whole joints have fled, and their bones
   decayed,
And dishes have broken been,
But old tom still follows the kitchen-maid,
And slyly licks up the cream.
Now, old tom cat, in his lonely days,
Shall joyously think of the past,
And a big leg of mutton, that never was
   touched,
Shall be food for our Tommy at last.

Fast creepeth he, though he hath no wings,
And a sly old dodger is he,
As under the garret window he sings—
Ain't you coming out tonight, love, to me?
Then slyly he creepeth the gutters all round,
And his old tail he joyously waves,
As his lady love from a garret he spies,
And he sings his amorous staves.

Those who rely on human companionship alone are diminished—beware of the landlord who bans cats!

ANON

The trouble with cats is that they've got no tact.

P. G. WODEHOUSE

Cats are smarter than dogs. You can't get eight cats to pull a sled through snow.

JEFF VALDEZ

The Cheshire Cat

The Cat only grinned when it saw Alice. It looked good-natured, she thought: still it had *very* long claws and a great many teeth, so she felt it ought to be treated with respect.

"Cheshire Puss," she began, rather timidly, as she did not at all know whether it would like the name: however, it only grinned a little wider. "Come, it's pleased so far," thought Alice, and she went on, "Would you tell me, please, which way I ought to walk from here?"

"That depends a good deal on where you want to get to," said the Cat.

"I don't much care where—" said Alice.

"Then it doesn't matter which way you walk," said the Cat.

"—so long as I get *somewhere*," Alice added as an explanation.

"Oh, you're sure to do that," said the Cat, "if you only walk long enough."

Alice felt that this could not be denied, so she tried another question. "What sort of people live about here?"

"In *that* direction," the Cat said, waving its right paw round, "lives a Hatter: and in *that* direction," waving the other paw, "lives a March Hare. Visit either you like: they're both mad."

"But I don't want to go among mad people," Alice remarked.

"Oh, you can't help that," said the Cat: "we're all mad here. I'm mad. You're mad."

"How do you know I'm mad? said Alice.

"You must be," said the Cat, "or you wouldn't have come here."

Alice didn't think that proved it at all;

however, she went on: "and how do you know that you're mad?"

"To begin with," said the Cat, "a dog's not mad. You grant that?"

"I suppose so," said Alice.

"Well then, " the Cat went on, "you see a dog growls when it's angry, and wags its tail when it's pleased. Now I growl when I'm pleased, and wag my tail when I'm angry. Therefore I'm mad."

"I call it purring, not growling," said Alice.

"Call it what you like," said the Cat. "Do you play croquet with the Queen to-day?"

"I should like it very much," said Alice, "but I haven't been invited yet."

"You'll see me there," said the Cat, and vanished.

Alice was not much surprised at this, she was getting so well used to queer things happening. While she was still looking at the place where it had been, it suddenly appeared again.

"By-the-bye, what became of the baby?"

said the Cat. "I'd nearly forgotten to ask."

"It turned into a pig," Alice answered very quietly, just as if the Cat had come back in a natural way.

"I thought it would," said the Cat, and vanished again.

Alice waited a little, half expecting to see it again, but it did not appear and after a minute or two she walked on in the direction in which the March Hare was said to live. "I've seen hatters before," she said to herself: "the March Hare will be much the most interesting, and perhaps as this is May it won't be raving mad—at least not so mad as it was in March." As she said this, she looked up, and there was the Cat again, sitting on a branch of a tree.

"Did you say pig, or fig?" said the Cat.

"I said pig," replied Alice; "and I wish you wouldn't keep appearing and vanishing so suddenly: you make one quite giddy."

"All right," said the Cat; and this time it vanished quite slowly, beginning with the end of the tail, and ending with the grin, which remained some time after the rest of it had gone.

"Well! I've often seen a cat without a grin," thought Alice; "but a grin without a cat! It's the most curious thing I ever saw in all my life!"

LEWIS CARROLL
FROM *ALICE IN WONDERLAND*

Cats have intercepted my footsteps at the ankle for so long that my gait, both at home and on tour, has been compared to that of a man wading through a low surf.

ROY BLOUNT, JR.

If you want to know the character of a man, find out what his cat thinks of him.

ANON

If man could be crossed with the cat it would improve man, but it would deteriorate the cat.

MARK TWAIN

Pussy cat, pussy cat, where have you been?
I've been to London to meet the Queen.
Pussy cat, pussy cat, what did you there?
I frightened a little mouse under her chair.

NURSERY RHYME

But I tell you, a cat needs a name that's
  particular,
A name that's peculiar, and more dignified,
Else how can he keep up his tail perpendicular,
Or spread out his whiskers, or cherish his
  pride?

> **T. S. ELIOT**
> **FROM "THE NAMING OF CATS,"**
> *OLD POSSUM'S BOOK OF PRACTICAL CATS*

When food mysteriously goes,
The chances are that Pussy knows
More than she leads you to suppose.

And hence there is no need for you,
If Puss declines a meal or two,
To feel her pulse and make ado.

> **ANON**

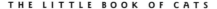

With cats, some say, one rule is true:
Don't speak till you are spoken to.
Myself I do not hold with that—
I say, you should ad-dress a cat.

> **T. S. ELIOT**
> **FROM "THE AD-DRESSING OF CATS,"**
> *OLD POSSUM'S BOOK OF PRACTICAL CATS*

You, who've rejected the pick of the dish
And flatly refuse to be stirred
By the mention of meat, if you know there is
   fish,
Or of fish, if you know there's a bird;
You who listlessly trifle and toy
With a dream of delicious kedgeree,
Are eating with every appearance of joy
A humble and innocent bumble bee.

> **ANON**

Two cats sat on a garden wall,
For an hour or so together;
First they talked about nothing at all,
And then they talked of the weather.

D'ARCY WENTWORTH THOMPSON
FROM *NURSERY NONSENSE*

Hey diddle, diddle, the cat and the fiddle,
 The cow jumped over the moon.
The little dog laughed to see such craft
 And the dish ran away with the spoon.

NURSERY RHYME

From "The Fable of the Young Man and his Cat"

A hapless youth, whom fates averse had drove
To a strange passion, and preposterous love,
Longed to possess his puss's spotted charms,
And hug the tabby beauty in his arms.
Racked with his passion, and in deep despair,
The youth to Venus thus addressed his prayer.

Delighted Venus heard the moving prayer,
And soon resolved to ease the lover's care,
To set Miss Tabby off with every grace,
To dress, and fit her for the youth's embrace...

But see how often some intruding woe
Nips all our blooming prospects at a blow!
Just on that instant from an inner house,
Into the chamber popped a heedless mouse.
Miss Tabby saw, and brooking no delay,

Sprung from the sheets, and seized the
   trembling prey.

    CHRISTOPHER PITT
    (AFTER ÆSOP'S FABLE OF VENUS AND THE CAT)

From "Milk for the Cat"

When tea is brought at five o'clock
And all the neat curtains are drawn with care,
The little black cat with bright green eyes
Is suddenly purring there.

At first she pretends, having nothing to do,
She has come in merely to blink by the grate,
But, though tea may be late or the milk may
   be sour,
She is never late.

    HAROLD MONRO

The Three Little Kittens

Three little kittens lost their mittens
And they began to cry,
"Oh, mother dear,
We very much fear
That we have lost our mittens."
"Lost your mittens!
You naughty kittens!
Then you shall have no pie!"

The three little kittens found their mittens
And they began to cry,
"Oh mother dear,
See here, see here!
See we have found our mittens!"
"Put on your mittens,
You silly kittens,
And you may have some pie."

ELIZA LEE FOLLEN

The Life's Companion

The Kitten and the Falling Leaves

That way look, my Infant, lo!
What a pretty baby-show!
See the kitten on the wall,
Sporting with the leaves that fall,
Withered leaves—one—two—and three—
From the lofty elder tree!...
But the kitten, how she starts,
Crouches, stretches, paws and darts!
First at one, and then its fellow,
Just as light, and just as yellow...
What intenseness of desire
In her upward eye of fire!
With a tiger-leap half-way,
Now she meets the coming prey,
Lets it go as fast, and then
Has it in her power again...
Such a light of gladness breaks,
Pretty kitten! from thy freaks,—
Spreads with such a living grace

O'er my little Dora's face;
Yes, the sight so stirs and charms
Thee, Baby, laughing in my arms,
That almost I could repine
That your transports are not mine...
Now and then I may possess
Hours of perfect gladsomeness,
—Pleased by any random toy;
By a kitten's busy joy,
Or an infant's laughing eye
Sharing in the ecstasy;
I would fain like that or this,
Find my wisdom in my bliss;
Keep the sprightly soul awake,
And have faculties to take,
Even from things by sorrow wrought,
Matter for a jocund thought,
Spite of care, and spite of grief,
To gambol with Life's falling leaf.

WILLIAM WORDSWORTH

The Cats of Kilkenny

There once were two cats of Kilkenny,
Each thought there was one cat too many;
So they fought and they fit,
And they scratched and they bit,
Till, excepting their nails
And the tips of their tails,
Instead of two cats, there weren't any.

TRADITIONAL LIMERICK

From "Cat-English"

It may seem funny, but my cat
Is learning English. Think of that!
For years she did all right with "meow,"
But that won't satisfy her now.

KINGSLEY AMIS

The Cat

You all day long, beside the fire,
Retrace in dreams your dark desire,
And mournfully complain
In grave displeasure, if I raise
Your languid form to pat or praise;
And so to sleep again.

You loved me when the fire was warm,
But, now I stretch a fondling arm,
You eye me and depart.
Cold eyes, sleek skin, and velvet paws,
You win my indolent applause,
You do not win my heart.

ARTHUR BENSON

When I play with my cat, who knows whether she is not amusing herself with me more than I with her.

MICHEL DE MONTAIGNE

I have a kitten, my dear, the drollest of all creatures that ever wore a cat's skin. Her gambols are not to be described, and would be incredible if they could. She tumbles head over heels several times together, she lays her cheek to the ground and presents her rump at you with an air of most supreme disdain, from this posture she rises to dance on her hind feet, an exercise she performs with all the grace imaginable, and she closes those various exhibitions with a loud smack of her lips, which for want of greater propriety of expression we call spitting. But though all cats spit, no cat ever produced such a sound as she does. For point of size she is likely to be a kitten always, being extremely small of her age, but time I suppose, that spoils everything, will make her also a cat. You will see her I hope before that melancholy period shall arrive, for no wisdom that she may gain by experience, and reflect hereafter, will compensate the loss of her present hilarity. She is dressed in a tortoiseshell suit, and I know that you will like her.

WILLIAM COWPER, FROM A LETTER TO HIS COUSIN LADY HESKETH, 1787

From "The Tortoiseshell Cat"

The tortoiseshell cat
She sits on the mat
As gay as a sunflower she;
In orange and black you see her blink,
And her waistcoat's white, and her nose is pink,
And her eyes are green as the sea.

PATRICK R. CHALMERS

A cat rolled up into a ball, or crouched with its paws folded underneath it, seems an emblem of repose and contentment. There is something soothing in the mere sight of it.

CHARLES H. ROSS

From "Pax"

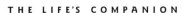

All that matters is to be at one with the
living God
To be a creature in the house of the God of
Life.
Like a cat asleep on a chair,
At peace, in peace
And at one with the master of the house,
with the mistress,
At home, at home in the house of the living,
Sleeping on the hearth, and yawning before
the fire.

D. H. LAWRENCE

Wonderful, wonderful is our life, and that of our companions! That there should be such a thing as a brute animal, not human! that it should attain to a sort of our society with our race! Think of cats for instance; they are neither Chinese nor Tartars, they neither go to school, nor read the Testament. Yet how near they come to doing so, how much they are like us who do.

HENRY DAVID THOREAU
JOURNAL

Our perfect companions never have fewer than four feet.

COLETTE

Inscribed in a London church after World War II in tribute to a cat who survived the Blitz.

On Monday, 9 September, 1940, she endured horrors and perils beyond the power of words to tell.

Shielding her kitten in a sort of recess in the house (a spot she selected only three days before the tragedies occurred), she sat the whole frightful night of bombing and fire, guarding her little kitten.

The roofs and masonry exploded, the whole house blazed, four floors fell through in front of her. Fire and ruin all around her.

Yet she stayed calm and steadfast and waited for help.

We rescued her in the early morning while the place was still burning, and by the mercy of Almighty God she and her kitten were not only saved, but unhurt.

She sights a Bird—she chuckles—
She flattens—then she crawls—
She runs without the look of feet—
Her eyes increase to Balls—

Her Jaws stir—twitching—hungry—
Her Teeth can hardly stand—
She leaps, but Robin leaped the first—
Ah, Pussy, of the Sand,

The Hopes so juicy ripening—
You almost bathed your Tongue—
When Bliss disclosed a hundred Toes—
And fled with every one—

EMILY DICKINSON

Sir Walter Scott's Cat

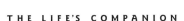

The cat assumed a kind of ascendancy among the quadrupeds—sitting in state in Scott's arm-chair, and occasionally stationing himself on a chair beside the door, as if to review his subjects as they passed, giving each dog a cuff beside the ears as he went by. This clapper-clawing was always taken in good part; it appeared to be, in fact, a mere act of sovereignty on the part of Grimalkin, to remind the others of their vassalage; which they acknowledged by the most perfect acquiescence. A general harmony prevailed between sovereign and subjects, and they would all sleep together in the sunshine.

WASHINGTON IRVING
FROM *ABBOTSFORD*

From "A Poet's Lamentation for the Loss of His Cat"

Whene'er I felt my towering fancy fail,
I stroked her head, her ears, her tail,
And, as I stroked, improved my dying song
From the sweet notes of her melodious
    tongue.
Her purrs and mews so evenly kept time,
She purred in metre and she mewed in rhyme.

JOSEPH GREEN

If I let her in and go on writing without
taking notice of her, there is a real
demonstration of affection for five minutes.
She purrs, she walks round and round me, she
jumps on my lap, she rubs her head and nose
against my chin.

MATTHEW ARNOLD

Ode on the Death of a Favourite Cat Drowned in a Tub of Gold Fishes

'Twas on a lofty vase's side,
Where China's gayest art had dy'd
    The azure flowers, that blow;
Demurest of the tabby kind,
The pensive Selima reclin'd,
    Gazed on the lake below.

Her conscious tail her joy declar'd;
The fair round face, the snowy beard,
    The velvet of her paws,
Her coat, that with the tortoise vies,
Her ears of jet, and emerald eyes,
    She saw; and purr'd applause.

Still had she gaz'd; but 'midst the tide
Two angel forms were seen to glide,
    The genii of the stream:
Their scaly armour's Tyrian hue

Thro' richest purple to the view
  Betray'd a golden gleam.

The hapless Nymph with wonder saw:
A whisker first and then a claw,
  With many an ardent wish,
She stretch'd in vain to reach the prize.
What female heart can gold despise?
  What cat's averse to fish?

Presumptuous Maid! with looks intent
Again she stretch'd, again she bent,
  Nor knew the gulf between.
(Malignant Fate sat by, and smil'd)
The slipp'ry verge her feet beguil'd,
  She tumbled headlong in.

Eight times emerging from the flood
She mew'd to ev'ry watery God,
  Some speedy aid to send.
No Dolphin came, no nereid stirr'd:
Nor cruel Tom, nor Susan heard.
  A favourite has no friend!

From hence, ye beauties, undeceiv'd
Know, one false step is ne'er retriev'd,
   And be with caution bold.
Not all that tempts your wandering eyes
And heedless hearts, is lawful prize;
   Nor all, that glisters, gold.

THOMAS GRAY

Pluto—this was the cat's name—was my
favorite pet and playmate. I alone fed him, and
he attended to me wherever I went about the
house. It was even with difficulty that I could
prevent him from following me through the
streets. Our friendship lasted, in this manner,
for several years.

EDGAR ALLEN POE
FROM "THE BLACK CAT"

Last Words to a Dumb Friend

Pet was never mourned as you,
Purrer of the spotless hue,
Plumy tail, and wistful gaze
While you humoured our queer ways,
Or outshrilled your morning call
Up the stairs and through the hall—
Foot suspended in its fall—While, expectant,
you would stand
Arched, to meet the stroking hand;
Till your way you chose to wend
Yonder to your tragic end.

Never another pet for me!
Let your place all vacant be;
Better blankness day by day
Than companion torn away.
Better bid his memory fade,
Better blot each mark he made,
Selfishly escape distress
By contrived forgetfulness,

Than preserve his prints to make
Every morn and eve an ache.

From the chair whereon he sat
Sweep his fur, nor wince thereat;
Rake his little pathways out
Mid the bushes round about;
Smooth away his talons' mark
From the claw-worn pine-tree bark,
Where he climbed as dusk embrowned
Waiting us who loitered round...

Housemate, I can think you still
Bounding to the window-sill,
Over which I vaguely see
Your small mound beneath the tree,
Showing in the autumn shade
That you moulder where you played.

THOMAS HARDY

Star Cats

The Aristocats
Felix the Cat
Fritz the Cat
Garfield

The Pink Panther
Sylvester
Tom (and Jerry)
Top Cat

Children's Classic Cat Stories

The Cat in the Hat
Puss in Boots
Dick Whittington
   and his Cat

Old Possum's Book
   of Practical Cats
Tale of Tom Kitten

Some Famous Cat-lovers

Raymond Chandler
Winston Churchill
Cleopatra
Colette
Doris Day
Ernest Hemingway
Edward Lear
Robert E. Lee

Leonardo da Vinci
Doris Lessing
Isaac Newton
Edgar Allen Poe
Cardinal Richelieu
Theodore Roosevelt
Queen Victoria
William Butler Yeats